THE AUDUBON SOCIETY POCKET GUIDES

A Chanticleer Press Edition

Stephen H. Amos
Assistant Director, Fairbanks Museum and
Planetarium, St. Johnsbury, Vermont

FAMILIAR MARINE MAMMALS

Alfred A. Knopf, New York

This is a Borzoi Book
Published by Alfred A. Knopf, Inc.

All rights reserved. Copyright 1990 under the
International Union for the protection of literary and
artistic works (Berne). Published in the United States
by Alfred A. Knopf, Inc., New York, and
simultaneously in Canada by Random House of Canada
Limited, Toronto.
Distributed by Random House, Inc., New York.

Prepared and produced by Chanticleer Press, New
York.
Typeset by Dix Type Inc., Syracuse, New York.
Printed and bound by Dai Nippon, Tokyo, Japan.
First Printing

Library of Congress Catalog Number: 90-052504
ISBN 0-679-72983-6

Trademark "Audubon Society" used by publisher under
license from the National Audubon Society, Inc.

Cover photograph: Killer Whale by François Gohier

Contents

How to Use This Guide

Marine mammals, creatures of great intelligence with astonishing agility in the water, have captured the imaginations of people throughout history. Utterly at ease in a world that is alien to us, they nonetheless lead lives that we find both understandable and compellingly original.

Coverage

This new guide covers 58 species of marine mammals native to North American waters. Some species are commonly observed, a few much more rarely seen. The seals, sea lions, and walruses live part of the time in the water and part of the time on sandy or rocky shorelines or on ice. The whales, dolphins, and porpoises spend their entire lives in the ocean. Some species can be seen in inshore waters, others require trips to open seas.

Organization

This easy-to-use guide is divided into four parts: introductory essays, illustrated accounts of the species, discussions of key aspects of these mammals' behavior, and appendices.

Introduction

As a basic introduction, the essay "Identifying Marine Mammals," describes the elements of identifying these sometimes elusive creatures by shape, behavior, color and pattern, size, range, and habitat.

The Marine Mammals	This section is divided into three parts. Part I contains 15 full-page color plates of seals and sea lions, plus the Sea Otter, the Walrus, and the Manatee. The photos are accompanied by text accounts covering interesting facts, identifying features, range, and habitat. Part II contains the photographs and accounts for 34 whales, dolphins, and porpoises. Part III contains paintings of nine species of rare whales.
Behavior	The behavior section contains two essays, the first on behavior patterns in the mammals included in Part I of the accounts, the second on characteristic behavior of whales, dolphins, and porpoises.
Appendices	Included in the appendices are a guide to the major groups of marine mammals, line drawings showing the anatomy of baleen whales and toothed whales, and drawings of diving sequences of some common whales. There is also a glossary of terms and an index.

Whether you are visiting the coast or venturing out to sea, this guide will help you to identify the intriguing, intelligent, and always appealing marine mammals that you might find there.

Identifying Marine Mammals

Nearly everyone is familiar, in a basic way, with whales, dolphins, walruses, and seals. These large, distinctive animals are the subject of poetry, films, art, documentaries, children's literature, and a host of other cultural representations. Trying to identify these creatures in the wild, however—in open water, or from a boat, when only a fleeting glimpse of a back or a fluke may be seen—can be extremely difficult. There are a number of species of dolphins, for example, that are distinguished only by minor variations in color or pattern. The beaked whales are rarely seen or accurately identified, even by researchers. Fur seals and sea lions may look alike to those who aren't familiar with their differences.

This guide covers all the species of marine mammals that occur regularly in North American waters. By reading the entries and studying the pictures, you will learn to recognize the features—such as shape, color, size, range, and habitat—that will help you identify marine mammals.

Shape To the untrained observer, one whale or seal may look very much like another. There are differences between individual species, however, that are fairly easy to spot if you know what to look for. Is the beak distinct from the slope of the head? Is the dorsal fin triangular or slightly hooked? What is the color of the coat? What is the shape of the tail fluke? Is there a visible spout when the whale surfaces? Answering these questions will help you to make an accurate identification.

Behavior We tend to think that all dolphins like to ride waves, or that all whales spout when surfacing. But these stereotypes are true only of some species. Each kind of marine mammal engages in particular types of behavior, which are the result of its environment, social life, physical needs, and other factors. Read the species entries and the essays on behavior to learn how to distinguish marine mammals by their activities.

Color and Pattern It can be quite difficult to identify marine mammals in the water using only color and pattern. Coloring in some species may change with age, or may differ between sexes. But colors and patterns may aid in identification when used along with other characteristics. Look for distinctive markings on the flukes, or unusual markings or textures on the body.

Size Whales are big—but, from a distance, the difference between a 30-foot or a 50-foot whale is not always

9

evident. Judging sizes accurately becomes a matter of experience. If you are on a whale-watching boat, determine the length of the vessel to use for comparison. If you are watching from shore, try to use a landmark of known size and similar distance to approximate the length. Many of the sizes listed in the entries are for full-grown adults, although size ranges are sometimes given. In some species of seals, the males are much larger than the females; the size for both sexes is given when there is an appreciable difference. Be sure to use the information about size along with other field characteristics in this guide when making an identification.

Range and Habitat   In identifying marine mammals, *where* you see an animal is almost as important as what you see. Within a certain range, many types of marine mammals prefer specific habitats. Recognizing these preferences will narrow the possibilities when you are searching for a particular species, or help you determine what you have found. Each entry gives specific information on the species' preferences in habitat and its range.

The more information that you have, the more likely it is that you can make a confirmed identification. Maintaining records and taking photographs of what you have seen is useful, because scientists are still determining migration patterns, feeding behaviors, pod or herd sizes, and distributions of marine mammals. Any unusual sightings should be documented and reported to the nearest oceanarium, aquarium, or to the National Marine Fisheries Service.

Finding Marine Mammals

Although marine mammals live throughout North American waters, they can be difficult to see and unpredictable in their movements. The vastness of the ocean provides a refuge for many of these magnificent creatures—and just as well. Many of the larger species have been hunted nearly to extinction, and even with protection, a number are still threatened.

Finding marine mammals can be a challenge. You are most likely to spot large whales in the open sea, although Gray Whales *(Eschrichtius robustus)*, Right Whales *(Eubalaena glacialis)*, and Humpback Whales *(Megaptera novaeangliae)* sometimes swim near shore, especially during their migrations. Bottlenosed Dolphins *(Tursiops truncatus)* have been known to enter estuaries, the lower reaches of large rivers, and even harbors. As their name implies, Harbor Porpoises *(Phocoena phocoena)* may be found in ports and other places close to shore. Cruising on an oceangoing vessel will increase your chances immeasurably, because many dolphins and porpoises enjoy riding the bow waves of these vessels. The seasons will also play a role in finding marine mammals. During the summer months, many of the seals and walruses congregate in large numbers at traditional breeding and pupping grounds. Gray Whales can normally be seen in lagoons off Baja California during the winter months. Commercial whale-watching expeditions have become popular on both coasts. On these trips, there is a good chance that you will see whales or dolphins.

Knowing a species' preferred habitats may also help; certain species can only be found in limited locales, making your search easier. Killer Whales *(Orcinus orca)* can generally be seen frequenting northern Pacific waters off Washington State. Sea Otters *(Enhydra lutris)* prefer California kelp beds, where there are plentiful food supplies in the waters below. Manatees *(Trichechus manatus)* are found in warm-water lagoons and tributaries, where they feed on water hyacinth. This guide details the habitat and range of most species of marine mammals occurring in American waters. Before heading out to search for marine mammals, read up on the preferences of the creature you are seeking.

If you should see a whale, dolphin, or porpoise, make careful notes on its characteristics: its coloring, the shape of the front portion of the snout, whether it has a dorsal fin, and its general behavior. Notice how a whale dives—whether or not it throws its flukes out of the water, and if the entire top of the head appears—and for large whales, note the shape and height of the spout. Make a rough sketch of what you see, or take a photograph. These records will be helpful when you try to identify the species using this guide.

Strandings of whales, porpoises, and dolphins along beaches occur all too frequently, and scientists have yet to determine the exact causes. Strandings may provide an opportune time for you to get a close look. If an animal is still alive, you can take some steps to help save it. First, try to contact local officials or the state Natural Resources department. Any regional aquarium or oceanarium will have established rescue procedures for strandings, and the staff may be willing to travel several hours if necessary. While waiting, place wet cloths over the animal's eyes, and attempt to shade it: cetaceans die very quickly when exposed to the sun's direct heat. Keep the animal's blowhole clear of any water—it can easily drown. Keep people away, because the animal may be in a state of shock, and noise and disturbance will certainly hinder its recovery.

Unfortunately, most strandings result in death. But if proper authorities are contacted, at least the animal may provide us with information about this strange and disturbing phenomenon.

Luck and patience are the most important factors in finding many marine mammals. When you least expect it—as you are walking along a sandy beach or standing on the edge of a rocky shoreline cliff—you may suddenly be gratified by the sight of one of these magnificent creatures. There is nothing that can quite compare.

PART I: SEALS, SEA LIONS, SEA OTTER, WALRUS, AND MANATEE

Northern Fur Seal *Callorhinus ursinus*

Fur seals are named for their dense, insulating underfur. More than a million Northern Fur Seals breed each year in the Pribilof Islands of the northern Pacific Ocean. Outside of mating season, these seals are great ocean travelers, migrating in some cases more than 6,200 miles. Extensively hunted in the early 19th century for their prized fur and blubber, these animals are now protected under the 1972 Marine Mammal Protection Act.

Identification Male 6'3"–7'3" long; 330–594 pounds. Female 3'8"–4'8"; 84–119 pounds. Bulls have enlarged neck, small head, pointed nose, large eyes, and long whiskers. Blackish above with grayish shoulders and reddish below. Females more streamlined; grayish above and reddish below. Very large flippers and tiny tail.

Habitat Most of the year at sea, coming to rocky island beaches to breed in summer.

Range Arctic Ocean to S. California, in winter. Summers on Pribilof Islands in Bering Sea and San Miguel Island off California.

Guadalupe Fur Seal *Arctocephalus townsendi*

This endangered eared seal was nearly hunted to
extinction: by 1892, only seven individuals were known
to exist. They proved tenacious; half a century later,
the known population had doubled to 14. Today, thanks
to heroic conservation efforts and continued protection
under the 1972 Marine Mammal Protection Act, the
world population stands at more than 1,000. This seal
breeds in rocky caves on islands, and the bulls
vigorously defend their harems both on land and in the
water.

Identification | Male to 6′3″ long; to 350 pounds. Female to 4′6″ long;
100 pounds. Pointed snout; long flippers. Brownish gray
above; silvery cast on tannish-gray head and neck.
Brownish black below, with rusty-orange sides. Male's
chest is lighter.

Habitat | Limited areas on rocky coastal islands.

Range | California's Channel Islands to Credos Island off Baja
California. Breeds on Guadalupe Island in summer.

Steller Sea Lion *Eumetopias jubatus*

The Steller Sea Lion is named for Wilhelm Steller, a naturalist who first described the species in 1741 as a "lion of the sea" for its golden-yellow pupils and loud roar. Commonly referred to as the Northern Sea Lion, this eared seal spends most of its time resting on rocky shores, except during rainy weather and high surf, when it takes refuge in the water.

Identification Male 8′10″–10′6″ long; to 2,200 pounds. Female 6′3″–7′3″ long; 600–800 pounds. Bull massive with large neck and forequarters; buff colored above, reddish brown below. Dark brown flippers. Cow uniformly brown, more streamlined, and usually ⅓ male's size.

Habitat Rocky shores and nearby shallow coastal waters.

Range S. Alaska, Aleutians, and Pribilof Islands to S. California.

California Sea Lion *Zalophus californianus*

The California Sea Lion—the familiar "seal" of zoos and circuses—was once hunted for oil and dog food, wiping out large populations. In the wild, these naturally playful and curious animals can often be observed tossing or balancing objects on their noses or chasing about in the surf. They attain speeds of 25 miles per hour in the water and can dive to 450', remaining submerged for nearly 20 minutes. Probably the most vocal wild mammal, the male barks long and loud, defending his harem on the summer breeding grounds.

Identification   Male 6'6"–8'2" long; 440–660 pounds. Female 5'–6'6"; 100–220 pounds. Slender, with high forehead. Buff to brown, appearing black when wet; color on head fades with age.

Habitat   Sandy or rocky island beaches; sometimes on mainland, in caves protected by steep cliffs.

Range   Vancouver to Baja California; Gulf of California. Preferred breeding grounds are islands from California's Channel Islands south through the Gulf.

Walrus *Odobenus rosmarus*

The Walrus is easily recognized by its large size and prominent tusks, which continue to grow throughout the animal's life. Except during the breeding season, these are sociable creatures, sometimes collecting in groups of more than 2,000 at resting and feeding spots. The bellow of breeding bulls may be heard a mile away; the males fight fiercely for their mates, incurring broken tusks and severe injuries.

Identification   Male 8'2"–11'10" long; to 1,650 pounds in N. Atlantic, to 2,783 in Pacific. Female 7'6"–9'6" long; 1,250–1,870 pounds. Yellowish to reddish-brown nearly hairless hide. Short, round head with many bristles on the muzzle. Two large tusks, 14" long in Atlantic bull and up to 40" long in Pacific individual. Cow's tusks somewhat shorter, narrower, and more curved.

Habitat   Along continental shelf of northern seas, particularly along edge of pack ice.

Range   Greenland to Hudson Bay; Chukchi Sea off NE. Siberia in summer and Bering Sea off SW. Alaska in winter.

Sea Otter *Enhydra lutris*

A member of the weasel family (which also includes minks), the Sea Otter has long been greatly prized for its pelt. By 1911, despite a treaty prohibiting uncontrolled hunting, the Sea Otter was presumed extinct throughout its range, but a small group had survived along the California coast. Today, about 1,000 live there, and the species is repopulating its historical range in the Aleutian Islands and southern coasts of Alaska. Sea Otters do not have a layer of blubber; their fine fur traps air and provides both insulation and buoyancy in the frigid waters.

Identification   Male 30″–72″ long; to 80 pounds. Dark brown; head and back of neck yellowish or grayish, turning white with age. Short tail, thickened at base and gradually tapered. Webbed feet; hind feet are flipperlike.

Habitat   Shallow coastal waters; in areas with kelp beds and large shellfish populations.

Range   Alaska to California.

Harbor Seal *Phoca vitulina*

Also called the Leopard Seal for its spotted coat, the Harbor Seal is the most readily observed earless seal in American waters. Widespread on both the Atlantic and Pacific coasts, Harbor Seals can be seen basking on the shorelines during low tides. They sometimes follow tides up coastal rivers, or follow fish runs for hundreds of miles upriver in the spring. Harbor Seals can dive up to 300' and remain submerged for nearly 30 minutes.

Identification   Male and female 4'–5'7" long; to 300 pounds. Usually tannish gray to brownish with dark spots above, and spotted ivory below, but varies among individuals.

Habitat   Coastal waters and mouths of rivers; may occur in some northern inland freshwater lakes.

Range   Hudson Bay to Carolinas; N. Alaska to California coastline.

Ringed Seal *Pusa hispida*

The smallest of the earless seals, the Ringed Seal spends most of its life beneath the ice in the frozen waters of the Arctic Sea, using its sharp-clawed flippers to dig and maintain air holes in the ice. At pupping time, it digs a long, narrow den in the snow next to its breathing hole, where the single pup is born. Both adult and young spend a great deal of time out of water at this time, making them extremely vulnerable to the polar bear, their principal predator. Formerly called *Phoca hispida*.

Identification Male slightly larger than female; 4′3″–5′3″ long and weighing up to 220 pounds. Coloring quite variable: brownish to blackish above with black marbling or streaking on the back; yellowish to white below, lightly spotted dark. Frequently light-colored, irregular, ringlike markings on the sides.

Habitat Extreme northern areas on land-fast ice.

Range Arctic waters from Alaska east to Labrador and Newfoundland.

Gray Seal *Halichoerus grypus*

The population of this large seal, once quite rare, is increasing. The Gray Seal has been heavily hunted throughout history, and was placed under protective law for some time. Unfortunately, a bounty has been placed on this species in Nova Scotia, because it damages the nets of commercial fishermen and is thought to eat too many of the fish that are harvested by man.

Identification　Male to 10′ long; to 640 pounds. Female slightly smaller, 7′6″ long and 550 pounds. Grayish to almost black above, and somewhat paler below. Squarish head with long and pronounced snout. Males neck often wrinkled.

Habitat　Along rocky coastlines and islands.

Range　Labrador south to New England, including Gulf of St. Lawrence.

Harp Seal *Pagophila groenlandica*

The Harp Seal, also known as the Saddleback Seal, has long been an important part of Newfoundland's economy. In the 1960s and early '70s, harvests claimed over 300,000 seals—and brought in many millions of dollars each year. Today, the annual harvest limits have been decreased to help the species recover. Harp Seals make yearly journeys of up to 6,000 miles, and they can dive up to 900′ deep and stay submerged for more than 15 minutes. The pups are born with snow-white baby fur known as lanugo; these coats were once in great demand, and many thousands of young Harp Seals were brutally clubbed to death.

Identification	Male 4′7″–6′7″ long; to 400 pounds; female slightly smaller. Grayish to yellowish white above, with harp-shaped black saddle on back. Belly silver with small dark spots.
Habitat	On or around drifting pack ice in Arctic waters.
Range	Arctic Sea from Hudson Bay to Gulf of St. Lawrence; west to mouth of Mackenzie River.

Ribbon Seal *Phoca fasciata*

The Ribbon Seal is named for the distinctive bands around its neck, rump, and flippers. It is usually solitary—resting, molting, and giving birth on pack ice, but otherwise spending most of its time in the open waters of the Bering Sea. Ribbon Seals can occasionally be found along the inshore water coastlines of the northern Pacific, but in the remainder of their range they are rarely seen.

Identification   Male slightly larger than female, to 6′ long; 200 pounds. Male dark brown with ivory-white bands around neck, rump, and base of flippers. Female grayish with indistinct bands.

Habitat   In the open seas and around Arctic ice floes.

Range   Arctic and Bering seas from N. Alaska to Aleutians.

Bearded Seal *Erignathus barbatus*

The beard and long tufts of flat bristles on its snout make the Bearded Seal easy to distinguish from other seals. This large seal does not migrate, and it is usually solitary except during the breeding season, when groups of up to 50 individuals may be observed together. Polar bears, man, and sometimes even walruses prey on this species.

Identification Male slightly larger than female, to 8′11″ long and 900 pounds. Uniformly gray to yellowish, with a distinctive beard and long, flat bristles on sides of snout.

Habitat Northern coastal waters and shallow seas of Arctic and along subarctic continental shelf up to 500′.

Range Alaska to Labrador, including Hudson Bay.

Hooded Seal *Cystophora cristata*

When angry or threatened, the male Hooded Seal inflates its hood—a distensible sac—to frighten its antagonists. Hooded Seals are highly migratory, sometimes straying as far south as Florida from their normal northerly range. During migration, they can frequently be found near Harp Seals, although the two species don't intermingle. Juveniles, known as "bluebacks" or "bluemen" for their bluish-gray coats, are highly sought after by the fur industry.

Identification   Male 6'7"–8'2" long; to 880 pounds. Female somewhat smaller, to 7' long and 400 pounds. Steel-gray above and paler below, with irregular blotches of brown or white on back. Hood is an elastic nasal sac; when inflated, stretches from nostrils to forehead. Wrinkled when deflated.

Habitat   Normally found along edge of Arctic pack ice in deep waters.

Range   Baffin Bay into Gulf of St. Lawrence; off coasts of Labrador and Nova Scotia. Absent from Hudson Bay.

Northern Elephant Seal *Mirounga angustirostris*

Elephant Seal bulls are highly territorial, inflating their nasal pouches and giving voice to long, resonant bellows that may be heard a mile away. They fight readily to defend their harems. The largest of all seals, this species was hunted nearly to extinction for its oil; in 1892, there were fewer than 20 individuals, and they were found only on Guadalupe Island. Conservation efforts and protective laws have helped the species to recover.

Identification Male 14'9"–21'4" long; to 7,700 pounds. Female ½ male's size; up to 11'6" long and 1,980 pounds. Male has great bulbous snout drooping over muzzle. Brown or gray above, lighter below. Hind flippers have 2 lobes and greatly reduced claws.

Habitat Temperate waters; subtropical sandy beaches during breeding and molting times.

Range Gulf of Alaska south to Baja California. Breeds on islands, from Farallons off California south to San Benito Island off Baja California.

Manatee *Trichechus manatus*

Also known as Sea Cows, Manatees are curious gentle creatures that take great delight in playing with and embracing each other. Early sailors' sightings of females floating in the water and nursing their single offspring may have given rise to the legend of the mermaid. Manatees were nearly wiped out in the early 20th century thanks to a sudden rage for "sea beefsteaks." These endangered mammals are now protected from hunting, but many are fatally injured by boat propellers. Others, lured from grazing grounds by the warm waters of power plants, starve to death.

Identification Up to 15′ long; 2,000 pounds. Torpedo shaped, with a broad head and deeply cleft upper lip bearing numerous stiff bristles. Front legs flipperlike, with 3 nails at end; no hind legs. Paddle-shaped tail. No external ear. Gray, appearing blackish when wet.

Habitat Shallow coastal waters, bays, rivers, and lakes, in water no colder than 46°F.

Range North Carolina to Florida and entire Gulf Coast.

PART II: WHALES, DOLPHINS, AND PORPOISES

Gray Whale *Eschrichtius robustus*

Watching Gray Whales in Baja California has developed into a flourishing seasonal tourist industry, helping tremendously to protect this endangered species. Gray Whales were known to early whalers as Devilfish because they fiercely defended their calves against enemies, including Killer Whales *(Orsinus orca)*, sharks, and whalers. Gray Whales feed by grubbing along shallow bottoms stirring up clouds of ocean sediment as they search for amphipod crustaceans.

Identification Up to 46′ long; body tapered toward both ends. Mottled gray; may appear uniformly slate-blue or white from surface. Narrowly triangular head, sloping steeply downward from 2 blowholes. Long mouth curves slightly upwards; 2–5 deep throat grooves. Back has low hump ⅔ of the way from snout to flukes. Serrated dorsal ridge.

Habitat Coastal waters; migrates close to shore, sometimes in deeper waters in summer. Calving in warm shallow lagoons.

Range Bering and Chukchi seas to Baja California.

50

Minke Whale *Balaenoptera acutorostrata*

The Minke is the smallest of all North American baleen whales. Members of this group have horny plates of baleen, or whalebone, hanging in two rows from the upper jaw; the baleen filters food from sea water. Also known as rorqual whales, baleen whales can often be seen approaching vessels or breaching.

Identification	Up to 33' long; rounded, tapered toward back end. Dark gray to black above; belly and underside of flippers white. Diagonal white band on flippers; sometimes with crescent-shaped marks on upper side of body before flippers. Flat, narrow, and pointed triangular-shaped rostrum; 2 blowholes on top of head before tall, hooked, dorsal fin. Ventral grooves end just behind navel.
Habitat	Open seas over continental shelf; sometimes also in bays, inlets, and estuaries.
Range	In Atlantic from pack ice to Lesser Antilles, including Gulf of Mexico. In Pacific from Bering and Chukchi seas to tropics.

Bryde's Whale *Balaenoptera edeni*

Whales have adapted to a strictly aquatic life by developing a streamlined, fusiform body. Their flattened tails, or flukes, and their dorsal ridges and fins, give whales increased mobility and speed in the water. Bryde's Whale commonly feeds on surface-dwelling crustaceans and schooling fishes, and it can often be found near oceangoing vessels.

Identification Up to 46' long; tapered toward tail. Dark, smoky gray upper body; undersides and front edges of flippers grayish white. Slightly arched but not sharply pointed snout; 3 median dorsal ridges on rostrum; 2 blowholes on top of head. Hooked dorsal fin with irregular notches along edge; ventral grooves extend at least to navel.

Habitat In offshore and inshore waters.

Range Virginia to Caribbean Sea, including Gulf of Mexico; extreme S. California to Gulf of Panama.

Blue Whale *Balaenoptera musculus*

Reckoned to be the largest animal ever, the Blue Whale can reach 98 feet in length and may weigh almost 200 tons. It feeds almost solely on massive amounts of a tiny shrimplike crustacean called krill, which abounds in relatively shallow waters. Whalers have severely reduced the world's population of this species, and it is close to extinction today. Sometimes called the Sulfur Bottom (because an accumulation of cold-water diatoms turns its belly yellowish), it can be recognized from afar when it spouts, sending up a high, oval cloud of mist.

Identification To 98' long; fusiform, tapering toward rear. Light bluish gray above, mottled gray or grayish white below; belly may be yellowish. Broad and flat rostrum, nearly U-shaped, with single dorsal median ridge and 2 blowholes on head. Small triangular dorsal fin located on base of tail. Ventral grooves extend at least to navel.

Habitat Open seas; sometimes in shallow inshore waters.

Range In Atlantic and Pacific oceans from Arctic Circle to Panama, including Gulf of Mexico.

Fin Whale *Balaenoptera physalus*

Fin Whales are sometimes observed leaping clear of the water—an incredible feat for so large an animal. They are also known as Razorbacks, for the ridge between their dorsal fin and tail, and Finbacks, for the large, hooked dorsal fin. Fin Whales feed chiefly on small fishes, pelagic crustaceans, and squid, which they strain from sea water using their horny plates of baleen.

Identification To 79′ long; rounded body tapering toward rear. Blue-black above, white below, with a grayish-white angled stripe leading from behind flippers to dorsal ridge. Right lower and upper lips may be white; left lips are dark. Snout V-shaped with single dorsal median ridge. Top of head flat, with 2 blowholes. Dorsal fin steeply angled, placed far back. Back distinctly ridged behind dorsal fin. Ventral grooves extend at least to navel.

Habitat In inshore and offshore waters.

Range Arctic Circle to Greater Antilles, including Gulf of Mexico; Bering Sea to Baja California.

Humpback Whale *Megaptera novaeangliae*

Humpbacks are famous for their mournful "songs"—an elaborate series of repeated vocalizations. The songs are apparently specific to populations and can change over time, with an entire group learning the new song. The baleen whales trap large numbers of krill and small schooling fishes in a "bubble curtain"—a net of air bubbles released while swimming in circles underwater. Individual Humpbacks can be recognized by the patterns on the flukes.

Identification   To 53′ long; body tapers rapidly to tail. Overall black, with undersides of flukes mostly white; belly sometimes white. Random fleshy protuberances on head and lower jaw; 2 blowholes; rounded projection on top of lower jaw. Very long flippers; front edges scalloped. Dorsal fin small, on hump on back. Flukes deeply notched, concave, scalloped. Spout wide, balloon shaped.

Habitat   Usually along coastlines; sometimes in open seas.

Range   Migratory. N. Iceland and W. Greenland to West Indies and Gulf of Mexico; Bering Sea to S. Mexico and Hawaii.

Right Whale *Balaena glacialis*

Early whalers thought that this species was the "right" whale to hunt—its slow movements made it easy to harpoon, and it stayed afloat after death. The baleen was used for corset stays; the rendered blubber produced oil for lamps, cosmetics, and other products. The result of such usefulness is sadly predictable: today the Right Whale is an endangered species. Individuals may be identified by the pattern of calluses on their heads. Formerly called *Eubalaena glacialis*.

Identification To 53′ long; rotund body. Mottled brownish black, with some white on chin and belly; yellowish calluses on head vary in number and size. Arched jaw curves upward; 2 large blowholes. No dorsal fin or dorsal ridge. Broad flukes with pointed tips; deep notch where flukes meet. Characteristic V-shaped spout.

Habitat Near shore in shallow water; sometimes in large bays.

Range Iceland to E. Florida, occasionally in Gulf of Mexico, rarely in West Indies; Gulf of Alaska and SE. Bering Sea to Baja California.

Beluga *Delphinapterus leucas*

Also known as the White Whale and the Sea Canary
(for the whistling sounds it makes), the Beluga is highly
gregarious, sometimes forming herds of thousands.
Native to the Arctic pack ice, its predators include
polar bears—which can pull a full-grown Beluga
through a hole in the ice—and Killer Whales. The docile
Beluga prefers shallow water, making it one of the few
species of whales successfully kept in captivity. Belugas
feed on fishes, squid, and bottom-dwelling crustaceans.

Identification   To 16′ long; extremely stout body tapering to a distinct
neck. Newborns brown, gradually lightening to pure
snow-white in adult. Head small with short beak. No
dorsal fin; narrow ridge of small bumps behind middle
of back.

Habitat   Shallow bays and river mouths; occasionally travels
upriver. Sometimes in open oceans.

Range   Arctic Circle to New Jersey; most abundant north of
St. Lawrence River. Gulf of Alaska and in Bering,
Chukchi, and Beaufort seas.

Narwhal *Monodon monoceros*

Once known as the Unicorn Whale for the prominent tusk in adult males, the Narwhal is a highly gregarious species distantly related to the Beluga. The Narwhal uses its tusk primarily as a weapon in territorial disputes, but the tusk is also useful in digging up clams, the Narwhal's preferred food, from the ocean floor. In addition, these whales eat squid, fishes, and crabs.

Identification   To 16' long; stout body. Dark bluish gray or brownish, with leopardlike spots on sides and back in adults. In adult males, 1 or 2 teeth emerge as long tusks from upper jaw. No dorsal fin; series of bumps 2" high along dorsal midline from middle of back to tail.

Habitat   Near shore in bays; around pack ice during the warmer months.

Range   High Arctic of W. North America, primarily Lancaster Sound and surrounding areas. Most abundant in central Arctic; uncommon in W. Arctic.

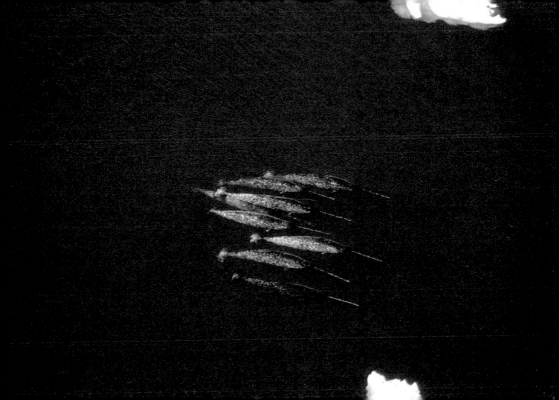

Rough-toothed Dolphin *Steno bredanensis*

Also known as the Black Porpoise or Goggle-eyed
Porpoise, the Rough-toothed Dolphin is most often seen
in offshore waters, where it feeds on squid and other
open-ocean members of the octopus family. The rough
surfaces of its teeth, which give this species its name,
are evident to the touch.

Identification   To 8′ long; rounded, torpedo-shaped body. Dark gray to
dark purplish on back with pinkish-white blotches
below; frequent white scars. White to pinkish-white
patch on one or both lips and tip of beak. Nearly conical
head has smoothly sloping forehead. Tall, hooked dorsal
fin.

Habitat   Offshore waters, usually off edge of continental shelf.

Range   Virginia to South America, including Gulf of Mexico;
central California to the tropics.

Bottlenosed Dolphin *Tursiops truncatus*

Some experts divide this species into the two races, Atlantic and Pacific. Bottlenosed Dolphins are naturally inquisitive; they often approach swimmers and also follow fishing boats to feed on scraps thrown overboard or creatures stirred up by the fishermen's nets. These intelligent dolphins are prodigious leapers and performers and hundreds delight observers with their acrobatics at zoos and aquaria. They are reknowned for their skills of echolocation and communication, but there is no evidence that they can "talk."

Identification To 12′ long; stout body. Back dark gray; sides lighter, shading to pink or white on belly. Individuals may vary from albino to nearly black. Well-defined short beak; prominent hooked dorsal fin near center of back.

Habitat Inshore waters including estuaries, shallow bays, and the mouths of freshwater rivers; sometimes further offshore.

Range Nova Scotia to Venezuela, including Gulf of Mexico; S. California to tropics.

Pantropical Spotted Dolphin *Stenella attenuata*

While the Pantropical Spotted Dolphin normally travels in herds of less than 100, groups of more than 1,000 have been reported. These dolphins are commonly observed near schools of yellowfin tuna—their principal food—and are often trapped along with the tuna in commercial nets. They can also be seen riding the bow waves of ocean vessels. Some taxonomists believe that this species is the same as the Atlantic Spotted Dolphin (*S. plagiodon*), which is the predominant form seen in Atlantic waters.

Identification	To 8' long; slender body with long, easily defined beak. Many contrasting spots, which may be hard to see from a distance. Very similar to the Atlantic Spotted Dolphin (*S. plagiodon*).
Habitat	Both inshore and offshore coastal waters in warm seas.
Range	Most common in eastern Pacific waters to Hawaii; sporadic sightings off western Mexico and in Caribbean.

Clymene Dolphin *Stenella clymene*

Known for a time as the Short-snouted Spinner Dolphin, the Clymene Dolphin has only recently been recognized as a distinct species from the Spinner Dolphin *(S. longirostris)*. It commonly rides the bow waves of oceangoing vessels and when leaping clear of the water, it spins—rotating its body rapidly along the long axis. The reasons for spinning are unknown; it may simply be done for pleasure.

Identification To 6'6" long; relatively small and slender. Dark gray to black above, with lighter sides and white belly. Dark coloring on back extends well down sides below dorsal fin; dark stripe narrows from flipper to eye. Moderately long beak pale on top, distinctly black tip and lips. Somewhat hooked, erect dorsal fin.

Habitat Open seas and deep coastal waters near islands.

Range New Jersey to Lesser Antilles.

Striped Dolphin *Stenella coeruleoalba*

Frequently found in herds of several hundred or more, the Striped Dolphin feeds primarily on fishes, squid, and crustaceans. Ocean travelers may observe these dolphins riding the bow waves of vessels, at times leaping clear of the water. Also known as the Meyer's Dolphin, Blue-white Dolphin, Gray's Dolphin, Streaker Porpoise, and Whitebelly.

Identification   To 9′ long; moderately stout. Dark gray to bluish-gray head and back; sides lighter gray; throat and belly white. Both sides of body have 1–2 black stripes extending from eye to flipper; another runs from eye to anus, with a small branch ending above and behind flipper. Black patch around each eye, connected to well-defined black beak. Distinctive light patch on side extends into dark area near hooked dorsal fin.

Habitat   Warm temperate and tropical waters beyond edge of continental shelf; warm water pockets in northern seas.

Range   Nova Scotia to Lesser Antilles, including Gulf of Mexico; Bering Sea to NW. South America.

Bridled Dolphin *Stenella frontalis*

The Bridled Dolphin is named for its markings around and behind each eye. It can often be seen riding the bow waves of oceangoing vessels, and it feeds on fishes, squid, and shrimp. In recent years, the scientific name *S. froenatus* has sometimes been applied to this species. The Pantropical Spotted Dolphin of eastern Pacific waters *(S. attentuata)* is considered by some to be a race of the Bridled Dolphin. Also known as Cuvier's Dolphin or the Bridled Spotted Dolphin.

Identification To 7′ long; moderately stout. Dark gray back, fading to lighter gray on sides and belly. Dark areas have light spots; light areas have dark spots. Side of head light gray, with distinctive black circle around eye. Broad, black stripe runs from mouth to flipper. Well-defined beak with white to pinkish lips. Hooked dorsal fin.

Habitat Coastal areas and islands; also offshore tropical waters.

Range Massachusetts to Lesser Antilles, including Gulf of Mexico.

Spinner Dolphin *Stenella longirostris*

Named for its habit of leaping clear of the water and rotating on its long axis, this dolphin often rides the bow waves of vessels. Spinner Dolphins may be found in large herds, feeding primarily on fishes and squid. Large numbers have been caught and killed in purse seine nets set by commercial tuna fishermen in tropical waters of the eastern Pacific. Modifications to the nets have reduced, but not eliminated, these fatalities.

Identification   To 7' long; slender. Dark gray to black above, with tan to yellowish-brown sides and white belly. Dark back runs parallel to lighter colored sides. Thick stripe from eye to flipper. Long, slender beak, dark on top with gray just behind black tip. Black lips. Dorsal fin gray, bordered by darker gray or black; erect and somewhat hooked, although in older males it may be triangular or tilted forward.

Habitat   Tropical oceanic and coastal waters.

Range   North Carolina to S. Brazil, including Gulf of Mexico; In Pacific, south of United States–Mexico border.

Common Dolphin *Delphinus delphis*

This abundant dolphin frequently travels in herds of more than a thousand. Common Dolphins ride the bow waves of oceangoing vessels for long periods, at times leaping clear of the water. Their playful habits and their evident joy strike a responsive chord in humans. Also known as the Hourglass Dolphin, Saddleback Dolphin, and White-bellied Porpoise.

Identification   To 8′6″ long; slender, tapering. Black to brownish-black back, cream to white chest and belly. Sides have distinct hourglass pattern of tan or yellowish. Well-defined dark beak may have white tip; 1 or more white stripes from jaw to flipper. Dorsal fin hooked to triangular with pointed tip; usually black, with gray at middle.

Habitat   Offshore waters over continental shelf near shelf ridges. Rarely seen in inshore waters.

Range   Newfoundland and Nova Scotia to N. South America; British Columbia to equator.

82

Fraser's Dolphin *Lagenodelphis hosei*

This very rare dolphin is believed to be related to both the genera *Lagenorhynchus* and *Lissodelphis*—thus the combined genus name, *Lagenodelphis*. Very little is known of the habits of the Fraser's Dolphin, although experts agree that it must be a relatively deep-diving species. A group of more than 580 individuals has been sighted. They tend to shy away from boats and are reported to be fast swimmers.

Identification To 8' long; moderately stout. Dark grayish blue above, white below; marked dark stripe from head to anus; similar overall to Striped Dolphin *(Stenella coeruleoalba)* but with shorter beak and smaller flippers.

Habitat Found in open, tropical, and warm temperate oceans.

Range Observed sporadically in our range in West Indies; principally in eastern Pacific.

Atlantic White-sided Dolphin *Lagenorhynchus acutus*

This dolphin is often observed in extremely large numbers by whale-watchers at sea. It is also known as the Jumper, for it's frequently seen leaping clear of the water surface. Atlantic White-sided Dolphins are somewhat wary of ocean vessels and usually will not ride bow waves. Scientists have recorded a variety of dolphin vocalizations, described as whistles, chirps, barks, and groans, that are believed to be methods of communication between individuals and between herds.

Identification To 9′ long; stout. Dark above and white below; sides marked with variable amounts of gray, tan, and white. Elongated areas of yellowish white to white extending from below dorsal fin to anus. Small but distinct black beak. Dorsal fin tall, noticeably hooked, pointed tip.

Habitat Cold offshore waters.

Range In Atlantic from S. Greenland to N. Virginia.

White-beaked Dolphin *Lagenorhynchus albirostris*

The White-beaked Dolphin is easily recognized by its distinctively colored beak. Like all other species of dolphins and porpoises, and many whales, the White-beaked Dolphin is an Odontocete—a toothed Cetacean. This species is also known as the Squidhound for its directed interest in squid, its primary food.

Identification   To 10′ long; stout body with gently tapering tail. Dark gray to black above, white to light gray on belly; sides have 2 grayish areas below dorsal fin. Distinctive white beak and tall dorsal fin.

Habitat   Offshore waters.

Range   Davis Straits and S. Greenland to Cape Cod.

Pacific White-sided Dolphin *Lagenorhynchus obliquidens*

Also known as the Lag, White-Striped Dolphin, or Hookfin Porpoise, this dolphin can frequently be found in herds numbering up to several thousand, feeding on a great variety of fishes and squid. The Pacific White-sided Dolphin is common in inshore waters near deep canyons along the Pacific Coast.

Identification To 7'6" long; cylindrical body with head tapering smoothly to shortened beak. Black above and white below, with white or light gray stripe beginning at forehead and continuing over head, along body on each side, and widening and curving towards anus, forming a distinctive light gray patch on flanks. Narrow black stripe runs from mouth to dark gray flippers; another dark stripe runs from flippers to dark area on flank. Dorsal fin tall, strongly hooked; dark on front, remainder light gray.

Habitat Offshore waters within outer edge of continental shelf. Also in deep canyons of inshore waters.

Range Aleutians and Gulf of Alaska to Baja California.

Risso's Dolphin *Grampus griseus*

Also known as the Grampus, Risso's Dolphin is most commonly observed in groups of a dozen or fewer, although it occurs infrequently in herds of several hundred or more. On some occasions, they ride the bow waves of ocean vessels, at times leaping high above the water's surface. They primarily eat squid but also feed on a number of fishes.

Identification   To 13′ long; stout, tapering abruptly toward narrow tail. Nearly black, with distinctive grayish-white areas on belly; numerous scars. Head lightens with age; flippers, dorsal fin, and flukes remain dark. Head bulbous, with V-shaped indentation on the front dividing this bump (or "the melon"). Tall, hooked dorsal fin near middle of back.

Habitat   Open temperate and tropical waters, following outer edge of continental shelf; in coastal waters where shelf edge is close to shore.

Range   E. Newfoundland to Lesser Antilles, including Gulf of Mexico; N. Washington to tropics.

Pygmy Killer Whale *Feresa attenuata*

Also known as the Slender Blackfish, the Pygmy Killer Whale can be belligerent when captured. It is known to feed on fishes and squids, but it also attacks and feeds on smaller marine animals. The Pygmy Killer Whale is not actually a whale but an ocean dolphin—like the larger but superficially similar pilot whales.

Identification
To 9′ long; relatively slender. Dark gray or black above; lighter sides, extending higher in front of dorsal fin. Small patch of white on underside; distinctive white markings around lips. Chin sometimes completely white. Rounded head with broad, receding lower jaw. No beak; teeth obvious in both jaws. Hooked dorsal fin near middle of back.

Habitat
Offshore in warmer waters.

Range
North Carolina to Gulf of Mexico and Lesser Antilles; in Pacific, found in tropical waters south of Mexico.

False Killer Whale *Pseudorca crassidens*

This medium-sized Odontocete is not nearly as aggressive as its cousin, the Killer Whale *(Orcinus orca)*. The False Killer Whale has been known to steal fish from commercial fishing lines, and it frequently approaches oceangoing vessels. False Killer Whales are strong swimmers, often leaping clear of the water despite their size. Strandings are frequent, especially in sandy bays and estuaries.

Identification To 19′6″ long; slender body. Black above and below with faint gray markings (possibly scars) on belly between flippers. Narrow head, with bulbous forehead —or melon—overhanging lower jaw. Tall, hooked dorsal fin; long flippers with hump along front edge.

Habitat Tropical and warm temperate seas.

Range Maryland to Venezuela, including Gulf of Mexico; Aleutian Islands and Prince William Sound of Alaska to N. South America.

Short-finned Pilot Whale *Globiocephala macrorhynchus*

Short-finned Pilot Whales are regularly observed in large herds; consequently, mass strandings occur all too frequently. These pilot whales feed on fish and squid, and have been reported to hang vertically in the water with their heads out, a behavior known as "spy-hopping." Off California, this species is sometimes given the scientific name *G. Scammoni*, and it is also called the Blackfish and the Pothead.

Identification   To 23′ long; stout. Black overall, with anchor-shaped gray patch on chin and gray area on belly. Light-colored, angled streaks may extend from sides of blowhole toward back; gray saddle behind dorsal fin. Short flippers. Distinctive low, hooked fin located far forward on back.

Habitat   Temperate and tropical waters from outer edges of continental shelf seaward; sometimes closer to shore.

Range   New Jersey to Venezuela, including Gulf of Mexico; reported in Delaware Bay. In Pacific from Gulf of Alaska to Guatemala.

Long-finned Pilot Whale *Globiocephala melaena*

The Long-finned Pilot Whale is closely related to the Short-finned Pilot Whale *(G. macrorhynchus)*, but can be distinguished by its more northern distribution and taller dorsal fin. Like its cousin, it is also known as the Pothead for its bulbous forehead—called a melon—resembling an inverted cooking pot. In the past, whalers drove Long-finned Pilot Whales ashore and slaughtered them for their oil. This practice is illegal today, but the species is quite prone to strandings.

Identification To 20′ long; stout. Black with gray markings on chin and belly; gray saddle behind blowhole in larger individuals. Pronounced melon on head; long flippers. Long, hooked dorsal fin placed well forward.

Habitat Offshore waters; may frequent inshore waters and bays during summer months.

Range Iceland and Greenland to North Carolina; possibly to Georgia.

Killer Whale *Orcinus orca*

Also known as Orcas, Killer Whales are ferocious predators. Feeding mainly on fishes, sea turtles, squid, and seabirds, they also attack seals and dolphins; groups have even been known to attack baleen whales, apparently out of aggression rather than hunger. Despite such unprovoked aggressive behavior, Killer Whales are still favorites for zoos and aquaria—the animals' beauty and great intelligence evidently outweighing their negative traits.

Identification   To 31′ long; stout. Males larger than females. Black with contrasting white, tan, or yellow below from mouth to anus, extending upward toward dorsal fin. White oval patch above and behind eye; light gray saddle behind dorsal fin. Broad head; mouth large with large, pointed teeth. Dorsal fin tall and erect in adult males; smaller and hooked in females and juveniles.

Habitat   Cooler coastal seas; large rivers and tropical waters.

Range   Arctic pack ice to Lesser Antilles in Atlantic; Gulf of Mexico; Chukchi Sea to equator in Pacific.

Northern Right Whale Dolphin *Lissodelphis borealis*

Northern Right Whale Dolphins are distinguished by their speed in the water. They sometimes ride the bow waves of oceangoing vessels, leaping clear of the water, belly-flopping, side-slapping, or flipper-slapping as they swim. They can often be found in cold waters in herds of more than a hundred, feeding on squid and fishes.

Identification   To 10′ long; slender body tapering to extremely narrow tail. Black with distinctive, variable white pattern on belly from chest to tip of tail, narrowing abruptly just behind flippers. Usually a white mark on tip of lower jaw. No dorsal fin.

Habitat   Temperate waters off outer edge of continental shelf.

Range   S. British Columbia to Baja California.

Harbor Porpoise *Phocoena phocoena*

The Harbor Porpoise, which loves to eat herring, is sometimes known as the Herring Hog. It is also called the Puffing Pig for the loud blow it produces when exhaling. Harbor Porpoises are wary creatures, perhaps because of their frequent unpleasant encounters with humans in inshore waters. They usually avoid boats. In addition to herring and other fishes, Harbor Porpoises feed on octopi and squid. At times these small cetaceans are hunted by large sharks and Killer Whales *(Orcinus orca)*.

Identification To 6′ long; chunky with rounded, blunt head. Dark brown or gray, fading to lighter gray on sides and often spotted in transition area. White belly extends up to sides in front of dorsal fin. Beak small, difficult to distinguish. Small, dark, triangular dorsal fin.

Habitat Subarctic or cold temperate waters; inshore waters such as bays, harbors, estuaries, and mouths of rivers.

Range Davis Straits to North Carolina. Gulf of Alaska and E. Aleutian Islands to S. California; infrequently in Chukchi and Beaufort seas.

Dall's Porpoise *Phocoenoides dalli*

Dall's Porpoise is also known as the Spray Porpoise for the "plume" of water that it produces when it moves quickly through the water. It is frequently observed riding a ship's bow waves. It feeds on squid, small crustaceans, and deep-sea fishes, and its predators include sharks, Killer Whales *(Orcinus orca)*, and man. Japanese fishermen hunt this species in the northern Pacific; many are also caught unintentionally in salmon nets.

Identification To 7′ long; extremely stout. Small head and tail flukes. Shiny black, sometimes with variable large, conspicuous, oval white patches on sides below dorsal fin, meeting on belly. Forehead slopes to short beak. Dorsal fin triangular; white at tip and black at base. Tail with distinct keel above and below.

Habitat Offshore waters and beyond edge of continental shelf; sometimes in deep inshore waters.

Range In Pacific from Pribilof Islands to Baja California.

Baird's Beaked Whale *Berardius bairdii*

Named for their distinct snouts, beaked whales generally inhabit offshore waters and are rarely seen by casual whale watchers. Baird's Beaked Whale is the largest of the 11 species of beaked whales native to North American waters. It dives deeply, feeding on squid, octopi, crustaceans, sea cucumbers, and a variety of deep-sea fishes.

Identification
To 42′ long; rotund. Slate-gray; may appear brownish. White splotches on undersides. Prominent, bulging forehead slopes toward long, cylindrical beak. Lower jaw extends beyond upper; paired teeth visible at tip. Single blowhole. Prominent, almost triangular dorsal fin, located more than ⅔ of the way from head. Flukes nearly straight, with no distinct notch.

Habitat
Deep offshore waters.

Range
In Pacific from Bering Sea to Baja California.

Cuvier's Beaked Whale *Ziphius cavirostris*

Also known as the Goosebeaked Whale or Ziphius, Cuvier's Beaked Whale is widely distributed along both coastlines. Thought to be strong swimmers and deep divers, Cuvier's Beaked Whales feed primarily on squid and deepwater fishes. They surface only briefly from the depths, a fact that makes them difficult for casual whale watchers to observe.

Identification | To 24' long; stout. Dark rust-brown, slate-gray, or fawn; lighter belly frequently covered with light blotches. Pale head, distinctly white in older males. Pronounced indentation just behind small head visible in profile. Mouth small, with an indistinct beak in larger individuals. Adult males have paired teeth at tip of lower jaw. Dorsal fin tall; closer to tail than head.

Habitat | Open temperate to tropical seas; also near shore.

Range | Massachusetts to West Indies, including Gulf of Mexico; S. Bering Sea to equator.

Blainville's Beaked Whale *Mesoplodon densirostris*

Also known as the Dense-beaked Whale or Tropical Beaked Whale, adult males of this species are easily recognizable because of the high arching contour at the corner of the mouth. Little is known of the biology of the Blainville's Beaked Whale, but we know that their diet is largely made up of squid.

Identification — To 17′ long; round, tapered body. Black to dark gray above, lighter below; sometimes blotched with grayish white. Distinct beak; head marked by prominent rise of lower jaw near corner of mouth; mouth has high arching contour in adult male. Teeth visible only on rise of lower jaw. Flattened area in front of blowhole; small dorsal fin, triangular to nearly hooked. Flukes rarely notched, occasionally bulging backward near center of back edge.

Habitat — Probably tropical and warm temperate offshore waters.

Range — Nova Scotia to Florida and Bahamas; Gulf of Mexico. Also off N. California.

114

Sperm Whale *Physeter catodon*

The familiar Sperm Whale has long been prized by whalers for a waxy substance called spermaceti, used in cosmetics; the head also contains fine oil. Sperm Whales primarily eat squid but also take a variety of fishes. Extensive hunting and a low birth rate (one calf every four years) have taken their toll: large populations are now scarce, and individuals of over 50 feet—like the albino Sperm Whale that was Melville's inspiration for *Moby Dick*—are rare.

Identification To 69′ long, with massive head. Dark brownish gray above; belly and front of head sometimes grayish. Blunt, squarish snout projects far beyond tip of lower jaw. Single blowhole far forward on head. Row of large teeth visible on each side of lower jaw. Distinct dorsal hump, followed by small ridges or bumps. Ventral keel. Flukes broad, triangular, with deep notches.

Habitat Temperate or tropical oceans; rarely in water less than 600′.

Range In Atlantic from Davis Straits to Venezuela; Gulf of Mexico; Pacific from Bering Sea to equator.

116

PART III: RARE WHALES

Sei Whale *Balaenoptera borealis*

This large baleen whale—named for its association with the sei fish, a Norwegian name for the pollock—is an opportunistic feeder, catching surface plankton, krill, squid, and small schooling fishes. Baleen whales have two blowholes on their heads and produce a visible spout or blow when exhaling. This fact provides whale watchers with a method of preliminary identification from a distance.

Identification To 62′ long; round, tapered toward back end. Dark, steel-gray upper body; grayish-white belly. Leading edges of flukes sometimes white. Slightly arched snout; rostrum somewhat blunt. Paired blowholes on head. Tall, strongly hooked fin. Ventral grooves on skin extend to midway between base of flippers and navel.

Habitat Temperate climates; near and offshore waters in open seas.

Range Arctic Circle to Venezuela, including Gulf of Mexico. In Pacific from Gulf of Alaska to Baja California.

Bowhead Whale *Balaena mysticetus*

This endangered baleen whale was extensively hunted for several centuries, first by the Basques and subsequently by other Europeans. Also known as the Greenland Right Whale and Great Polar Whale because of its range, it has highly arched jaws in a massive head. Bowheads feed primarily on small crustaceans, which they usually skim and filter from near the surface. They are sometimes known to leap nearly out of the water.

Identification To 65′ long; in adults, top of head and back form 2 separate humps. Mostly black; chin has large splotch of white with grayish-black spots. Highly arched jaws; smooth head with 2 widely spaced blowholes that create 2 distinct spouts. No dorsal fin. Flukes broad with pointed tips; deep notch where flukes meet.

Habitat Around pack ice, often in shallow waters.

Range Off E. Greenland, Davis Straits, James Bay, and adjacent waters; also in Bering, Chukchi, and Beaufort seas.

122

Northern Bottlenosed Whale *Hyperoodon ampullatus*

The Northern Bottlenosed Whale is a deep diver and is thought to be able to remain submerged for more than two hours—longer than any other marine mammal. Like Sperm Whales *(Physeter catodon)*, Northern Bottlenosed Whales have spermaceti in the forehead. As the large populations of the Bowhead Whale *(Balaena mysticetus)* were becoming depleted, hunters turned to the Northern Bottlenosed for their profits.

Identification   To 32′ long; robust. Brownish, often lighter below; light blotches form on back and sides with maturity. Juveniles may be chocolate-brown; large individuals may have white head. Bulbous forehead with blowhole in indented area behind it. Narrow and cylindrical beak. Dorsal fin hooked; flukes have no distinct notch.

Habitat   Deep Arctic waters; offshore in cold temperate waters more than 600′.

Range   In Atlantic from Davis Straits and off Hudson Straits to Rhode Island.

North Atlantic Beaked Whale *Mesoplodon bidens*

Also known as the North Sea Beaked Whale or Sowerby's Beaked Whale, this species prefers offshore waters and is a rare treat for the casual whale watcher. It makes long, deep dives for food, largely squid. Little is known of the habits or physiology of many of the beaked whales, and the function of their beaks has not been determined, although scientists speculate that they may be used for catching and grasping food.

Identification To 16′6″ long; may reach 18′ or more. Long, tapered body. Dark gray above and lighter below; numerous light spots. Moderately long beak; pronounced bulge in front of single blowhole. Forehead slightly concave; teeth visible in lower jaw. Dorsal fin, halfway along back, varies from hooked to triangular. Flukes not notched; rear edges may be curved inward.

Habitat Offshore waters; sometimes nearer shore when feeding.

Range In Atlantic from pack ice to New England.

Hubb's Beaked Whale *Mesoplodon carlhubbsi*

The Hubb's Beaked Whale is a "new" species—it was first recognized in 1963. It is thought to be a deep diver, feeding on squid and small fishes in the mid-water regions of the Pacific Ocean. Many deep-diving whales must rest on the surface to ventilate their lungs fully and restore proper oxygen levels before attempting to dive again.

Identification To 17'6" long; round, tapered. Small head and narrow tail. Black, sometimes deeply scarred, with distinctive white patch on top of head. Forehead slopes into prominent beak. Single, substantial tooth visible on each side of lower jaw at midpoint of mouth in adult males. Mouthline forms S-shaped curve. Dorsal fin hooked. Flukes are notched.

Habitat Upper layers of open seas.

Range In Pacific from British Columbia to S. California.

Ginkgo-toothed Beaked Whale *Mesoplodon ginkgodens*

Also known as the Japanese Beaked Whale, the Ginkgo-toothed Whale has only recently been described. It is named for the teeth of the adult male, which are shaped like the leaf of the ginkgo tree. Members of the genus *Mesoplodon* are sometimes called cowfish.

Identification To 16' long; round, tapered body. Appears black above and lighter below. Belly and sides can show oval, white scars. Females may have light-colored heads. Smoothly sloping forehead, with prominent beak. Mouth line curves upward about midway between snout tip and eye. Single, flattened tooth visible in males. Triangular or hooked dorsal fin, nearer tail than head. Flukes not notched.

Habitat Probably the upper layers of temperate water in open seas.

Range In Pacific near San Diego, California, and in Baja California; possibly more widespread.

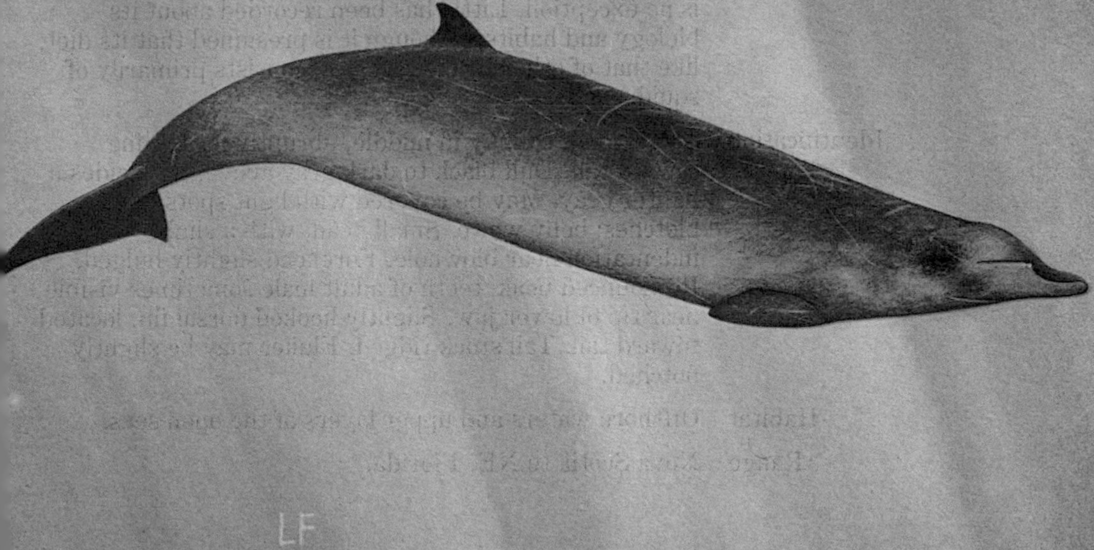

True's Beaked Whale *Mesoplodon mirus*

Beaked whales, as a group, are poorly understood in relation to other whales, and the True's Beaked Whale is no exception. Little has been recorded about its biology and habits, although it is presumed that its diet, like that of other beaked whales, consists primarily of squid.

Identification To 17' long; chunky in middle, abruptly narrowing toward tail. Dull black to dark gray above, with sides a lighter gray. May be covered with light spots or blotches; belly white. Small head, with a slight indentation near blowhole. Forehead slightly bulged. Pronounced beak; teeth of adult male sometimes visible near tip of lower jaw. Slightly hooked dorsal fin, located toward tail. Tail stock ridged. Flukes may be slightly notched.

Habitat Offshore waters and upper layers of the open seas.

Range Nova Scotia to NE. Florida.

Stejneger's Beaked Whale *Mesoplodon stejnegeri*

Also known as the Bering Sea Beaked Whale or the Saber-toothed Whale, the Stejneger's Beaked Whale is only known from stranded individuals. Males of this species may be covered with scars inflicted by other males during dominance disputes and mating seasons. Like other beaked whales, it probably feeds primarily on squid.

Identification To 17'6" long; round, tapered. Largely grayish brown above, lighter below, with light brush marks extending up sides behind head, on neck, and around mouth. Oval, white scars visible on flanks of adult males. Well-defined beak, with paired teeth emerging from prominent arches of lower jaw. Hooked dorsal fin, placed below middle of back. No notch on tail fluke.

Habitat Upper layers of open subarctic and cold temperate seas. Also found near islands in deep water.

Range In Pacific from S. Bering Sea to California.

Pygmy Sperm Whale *Kogia breviceps*

Like its close relative the Dwarf Sperm Whale *(K. simus)*, the Pygmy Sperm Whale has a strong receding jaw and is easily distinguished from other cetaceans by its exceptionally short rostrum. The Pygmy Sperm Whale is frequently stranded on beaches of the southeastern United States. It feeds on squid, crabs, shrimp, and some fishes in deep offshore waters. When disturbed, it may discharge a cloud of dark reddish-brown fluid to confuse would-be predators.

Identification To 12' long; stout body tapers abruptly toward tail. Dark steel-gray back; sides lighter gray. Dull white belly. Squarish head, with light gray, crescent-shaped mark on each side. Single blowhole, back from snout; 10–16 large, pointed teeth in each side of lower jaw. Small, hooked dorsal fin on back half of body.

Habitat Deep, offshore waters; close to shore during calving season.

Range Nova Scotia to Greater Antilles, including Gulf of Mexico; Washington to Baja California.

136

MARINE MAMMAL BEHAVIOR: PART I

Seal, Sea Lion, Walrus, Sea Otter, and Manatee Behavior

Sea Otters, Manatees, sea lions, walruses, and seals are among the most interesting mammals to watch. All except the Manatee have a remarkable ability to ad~ both land and sea; many of their actions seem *d* playful and sometimes almost human. These aquatic mammals form quite a varied group. Sea Otters *(Enhydra lutris)* are the only marine mammals in the weasel family, and Manatees *(Trichechus manatus)* are the only member of their family in North American waters. Sea lions and seals are divided by scientists into two distinct groups, eared seals and earless seals, that are thought to have descended from different ancestors. Eared seals—which include the Northern Fur Seal *(Callorhinus ursinus)*, the Guadalupe Fur Seal *(Arctocephalus townsendi)*, the Steller Sea Lion *(Eumetopias jubatus)*, and the California Sea Lion *(Zalophus californianus)*—have small but noticeable external ears, long and slender bodies, and supple forelimbs. Because their hind flippers can rotate forward under their bodies, and their long fore flippers can be turned out at right angles at the wrist, eared seals can propel themselves on all fours on land. Their normal gait

A Sea Otter and pup float comfortably.

resembles that of a dog, but they can also manage a kind of gallop. The eared seals are less specialized for life in the water than the earless and more agile on land. The Walrus *(Odobenus rosmarus)* evolved from an ancestral eared seal, but it has no external ears.

Earless seals, sometimes called true seals, include the Harbor Seal *(Phoca vitulina)*, the Ribbon Seal *(Phoca fasciata)*, the Ringed Seal *(Pusa hispida)*, the Harp Seal *(Pagophilia groenlandica)*, the Bearded Seal *(Erignathus barbatus)*, the Hooded Seal *(Cystophora cristata)*, and the Northern Elephant Seal *(Mirounga angustirostris)*. The most widespread of the aquatic carnivores, they have no external ears, merely small orifices. Their hind flippers are fixed in a backward position, limiting them to aquatic use. Earless seals are clumsy on land and they prefer ice.

Family Life   Sea Otters are highly aquatic—they eat, sleep, mate, and give birth in the water. Their flipperlike hind legs make them clumsy on land; they go ashore only when storms make their preferred habitat unsafe. Female Sea Otters give birth to one, or sometimes two, pups in

Manatees congregate in family groups

the spring. The pups are born with their eyes open and with insulating fur and teeth—fitted out for life in the water. They are weaned after a year, but they may stay with their mothers even after the birth of a new pup. Female Sea Otters are quite maternal; they float on their backs to let their offspring nurse, nap, or play on their chests. To protect their pups from predators such as Killer Whales *(Orcinus orca)* and sharks, mothers tuck them under a foreleg and dive for safety.

Surprisingly, the Manatee's closest evolutionary ties are with the hoofed mammals, particularly the elephants. Manatees are somewhat social; they congregate in warm water and play together when they meet. Manatees have been seen embracing each other with their flippers and pressing their lips together in an underwater "kiss." They move the hind ends of their streamlined bodies to propel themselves, using their flippers and tail to steer. They can hang in the water at rest, or lie on the bottom. Female Manatees produce one pup every two years. The birth takes place underwater, after which the mother places the newborn

A California Sea Lion nursing its pup

144

on her back and lifts it out of the water. Within an hour, she gradually immerses the pup again. Nursing is also accomplished underwater.

Eared seals remain at sea for most of the year, but they come to land—or sometimes ice—to breed. The males arrive first at traditional breeding grounds to establish their territory. Each attracts a harem of up to several dozen females. (Male California Sea Lions attract loose harems of up to 20 females.) Female eared seals, which are much smaller than the males, give birth easily. Their pups begin to suckle less than two hours after birth, and they enter the water about two weeks later, quickly becoming proficient swimmers. They learn to eat fish before they are completely weaned; weaning occurs at about one year. Pups can recognize their mothers' voices.

Earless seals are generally monogamous, pairing off during the breeding season (although Harbor Seals from coastal regions can be promiscuous). The Ribbon Seal, a solitary species, breeds in the spring and gives birth 11 months later on pack ice. The single calf is born

A Sea Otter whacks a clam on a stone to open it.

146

covered with white woolly fur, called lanugo, which it sheds after a month. Harp Seals mate in the water. The bulls emit a musky odor during the breeding season; they congregate between ice floes to court females.

Feeding Aside from primates, the Sea Otter is the most efficient tool user among the mammals. When it dives to the bottom of the ocean for its food (it prefers abalone, sea urchins, crabs, mussels, and fishes), it also picks up a rock. The animal resurfaces, floats on its back with the rock on its belly, and raps the shell of its food on the rock to get at the meat. (You can frequently locate Sea Otters in their preferred kelp-bed habitats by the loud, rapid tapping sound they make during these shellfish meals.) The Sea Otter's high metabolic rate allows it to consume up to $\frac{1}{5}$ of its body weight in food each day.

Unlike the other marine mammals discussed here, Manatees are strictly vegetarian. They browse at night on aquatic vegetation, grasping it in their lips and their bristles and holding it in their flippers. Manatees perform a very important service by eating large quantities of water hyacinth, a highly problematical

Supple-limbed Steller Sea Lions entering the water

introduced plant that is now clogging southern waterways. The animals can consume up to 100 pounds of this troublesome weed each day.

Among the eared seals, the Steller Sea Lions eat a variety of fishes and shellfish—including blackfish, rockfish, greenling, salmon, squid, clams, and crabs. They generally feed at night in waters less than 600 feet deep and within 10 or 15 miles of shore. Northern Fur Seals hunt at night for fishes and squid, which come closer to the surface at this time, as well as for small marine mammals and seabirds resting on the water. During daylight hours, they rest and groom their fur. California Sea Lions feed on a variety of fishes (which they decapitate before eating), squid, and abalone.

Earless seals may dive deeper to find their preferred foods. The diet of Harbor Seals consists principally of fishes, with squid, clams, octopus, crabs, crayfish, and shrimp making up the remainder. For many years, there was a bounty placed on these seals because of the damage they did to the nets of commercial fishermen as they hunted for food. Gray Seals commonly gather in

Male Northern Fur Seals guard their harems

groups, diving up to 480 feet and staying submerged up to 20 minutes while feeding on bottom-dwelling fishes such as pollock, cod, flounder, and whiting. Harp Seals eat small prawns and fishes—especially schooling capelin and herring. The Ribbon Seal feeds on such fish as pollock, capelin, sculpin, and polar cod, and occasionally eats shrimp and octopus. Bearded Seals use the sensitive bristles on their snouts and their sharp claws to locate and dig up whelks, clams, crabs, or octopus, their primary foods. Occasionally they feed on bottom-dwelling fishes. Hooded Seals dive deeply to locate their preferred foods, which include mussels, starfish, squid, octopus, and various fishes such as herring and cod. Northern Elephant Seals eat primarily fish, including hagfish and small sharks.

Walruses may dive up to 300 feet deep and stay submerged for nearly half an hour in search of mollusks, especially clams, and crustaceans, using their long tusks to unearth them. Sometimes they prey on seals and scavenge on small, dead whales.

A herd of Walruses on a rocky shore.

Herding   Most aquatic mammals gather in herds at some point in the year. Sea Otters form groups of up to 100 individuals, congregating in kelp beds, where both sexes rest together. Manatees do not form herds; they live in small family units of male, female, and one or two calves. They do congregate during winter months in warm water. Most, if not all, eared and earless seals and walruses join together at some time. During migration or feeding they form groups known as herds; during the breeding season they mass in large "rookeries" along isolated islands and shores. The population of these rookeries may number in the tens of thousands, depending on the species. Breeding males will ferociously defend harems of sexually receptive females, continuing to defend their territories through the summer, until the pups have been weaned. Some species of seals have special methods of distinguishing themselves during herding. In particular, the male Hooded Seal has an inflatable hood—part of its nasal cavity—that it can blow up at will. This grotesque appendage is used to threaten other males or to attract females during courtship displays.

A male Hooded Seal with its "hood" extended

MARINE MAMMAL BEHAVIOR: PART II

Whale, Dolphin, and Porpoise Behavior

Whales, dolphins, and porpoises, which are known collectively as cetaceans, are carnivorous, aquatic mammals that never leave the water at any stage of their lives. Like most other mammals, they are warm-blooded, have hair (or at least bristles) on their body at some stage in their life, maintain a constant body temperature, and bear their young alive. Experts generally agree on the use of the term "whale" for the largest cetaceans, but usage of the terms "dolphins" and "porpoises" is still somewhat inconsistent. Cetaceans occur in all seas and in certain fresh waters. Because they live their entire lives in the water, cetaceans are difficult for scientists to study, and many aspects of their behavior are still a mystery to mankind. Certain specific behavior patterns are examined here, with photographs showing the specific actions that are discussed.

Spouting, or Blowing

Breathing presents a special challenge for marine mammals, and particularly for deep-diving cetaceans such as whales. Unlike fish, which use their gills to

The Sperm Whale, with its single blowhole, has a distinctive spout.

extract oxygen from water, whales must come periodically to the surface of the water for air. In the few seconds during which they surface, they must expel the moist, used air from their lungs through their blowholes and take in fresh air. It is the pressurized exhalation, visible when the moisture in it condenses into white steam, that is referred to as spouting, or blowing. The traditional shout "Thar she blows!," given when a whale was sighted from a whaling vessel, was inspired by its spouting. The shape of many species' spout is characteristic, so it offers a good clue to identification for whale watchers.

Feeding Whales are divided into two groups, baleen whales and toothed whales, each with very different feeding habits. Baleen whales, also called mysticetes, include the Right Whale *(Balaena glacialis)*, the Gray Whale *(Eschrichtius robustus)*, and the Fin Whale *(Balaenoptera physalus)*. They have dozens of plates of baleen ("whalebone") hanging from their upper jaws. Baleen is a skin growth, somewhat comparable to hair,

A Humpback Whale feeds at the surface, straining seawater through its baleen plates

claws, or scales. It was greatly prized during the 19th century for its strength and flexibility and was used for women's corset stays. The whales take in gallons of ocean water and then strain it out through the baleen, capturing in the process many tons of tiny fishes, plankton, crustaceans, or krill, for the whale to eat. Baleen whales have two blowholes on top of their heads, through which they spout, or blow. Most baleen whales feed by skimming slowly near the surface of the water. Others swim at a faster rate, gulping large mouthfuls of water and expelling it—minus the food it contained—through the baleen.

Toothed whales, or odontocetes, include the Sperm Whale *(Physeter catodon)*, beaked whales (family Ziphiidae), the Beluga Whale *(Delphinapterus leucas)*, the Narwhal *(Monodon monoceros)*, the dolphins (Delphinidae), and the porpoises (Phocoenidae). These cetaceans have teeth, although the number varies greatly. Some have only a single tooth in each side of the lower jaw, while others have 65 or more in each side of both jaws. Toothed whales have only one

Podding Narwhals in icy Arctic waters

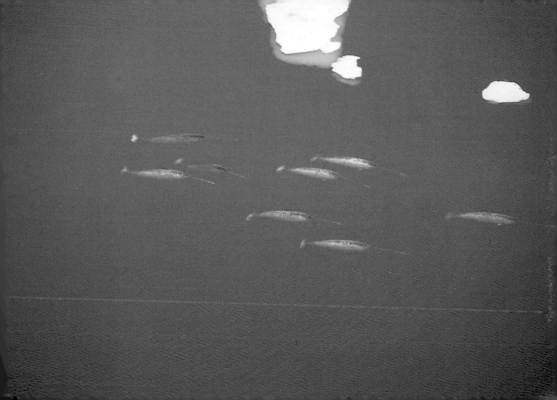

blowhole and no baleen. The Sperm Whale and beaked whales feed largely on squid.

Podding   Herding behavior, called podding when it refers to whales and dolphins, may be observed in many species of marine mammals, particularly during the breeding season and migration. Each fall, whales travel together to their traditional breeding locations. Gray Whales may travel up to 6,000 miles to reach their only known breeding ground, a shallow-water lagoon along the coast of Baja California in Mexico. There they assemble in large pods, awaiting the birth of the year's offspring. Whales and dolphins may also form pods while searching for food. Killer Whales *(Orcinus orca)* frequently travel in hunting packs of a dozen or more individuals, while Beluga Whales may be found by the thousands in the shallow tributaries of their Arctic homes, searching for fish during migration season.

Porpoising   Porpoises are not the only marine mammals that "porpoise," or move in and out of the water in a series of high-speed leaps. Many cetaceans, including whales and dolphins, as well as seals, sea lions, and some

Atlantic Spotted Dolphins "porpoising."

penguins, can be observed porpoising. No one knows exactly why these animals jump out of the water in this fashion. One theory holds that the animals can attain greater momentum and speed through this kind of motion. A group of porpoises, whales, or dolphins sometimes porpoise together, causing a splash that may help corral schools of fish, making it easier for the group to feed. Porpoising may also allow an animal to take a quick breath of air or to orient itself by getting a quick look at its surroundings. In smaller species, porpoising may be an important method of defense. Many species are known to pod and begin porpoising when a predator is near, confusing aquatic carnivores such as Killer Whales and sharks, who usually single out their prey and then chase it down. This group porpoising makes a successful capture more difficult.

Family Life   Many species of whales exhibit elaborate courtship rituals involving aquatic arabesques. The mating of whales usually takes place near the surface of the water, and in the early morning. Whales have three different basic mating methods. Some species, including

A Beluga calf stays close to its mother.

the Humpback Whale and the Bowhead Whale, mate while facing each other with their heads pointing up out of the water. Other species, including the Gray Whale, have been observed with one female being surrounded by three males; one male is assisted by the two others, who in turn also mate with the female. Some species mate while swimming side by side, with their bellies toward each other. The actual mating takes only a couple of seconds, but the courtship process may last considerably longer. Some researchers have suggested that the "singing" of the Humpback may be a form of sexual display. Whales generally give birth every other year. The large baleen whales have a gestation period of 11 months, after which a single calf is born. Toothed whales, dolphins, and porpoises generally give birth to one or more calves after a year's gestation, but frequently only one calf survives. Large beaked whales carry their young for 16 months.

Newborn whales arrive tail first. They are well developed—smaller editions of their parents—and are

When breaching, a Humpback Whale hurls its entire body out of the water

surprisingly large, weighing as much as two tons. Nursed by their mothers for up to a year, they grow rapidly. Whales generally give birth every other year. Mothers are strongly attached to their offspring, protecting them with their flippers and using distraction display techniques to draw the attention of predators away from the calves.

Breaching

Many species of whales, dolphins, and porpoises can be seen leaping clear of the water, a behavior known as breaching. Breaching is a spectacular act that never fails to impress people fortunate enough to see it. There are many theories about its function.

Many marine mammals have external parasites, including small crustaceans known as copepods, attached to their skin. Parasitic copepods, which may be as large as a foot across, burrow their heads under the host's skin to feed on its blood. One theory about breaching is that the force with which a whale, dolphin, or porpoise hits the water after a breach may help to

A breaching Atlantic Spotted Dolphin can achieve a spectacular height.

dislodge some of these irritating parasites. Breaching may also serve as a means of communication. The loud splash made by a belly-flopping whale can be heard for great distances underwater, where sound travels more readily than in air. By breaching, a whale may make its presence known to another individual quite far away. Although larger whales have relatively poor eyesight, the smaller cetaceans, such as dolphins, may use breaching as a way to observe the world above the water, especially in inshore waters where landmarks are visible. Cetaceans are known to be very intelligent; breaching may help them locate feeding, resting, or traditional breeding areas. Finally, breaching may be simply fun. Many species of cetaceans are known to play; breaching could be a spectacular form of recreation.

Spy-hopping

Spy-hopping, referred to as "pitchpoling" by some sailors, is performed by a number of cetaceans, from the larger whales to the smaller dolphins. Using their muscular tails, they lift their heads out of the water, a

A Killer Whale "spy-hopping," taking note of its surroundings

whale's form of treading water. Some authorities believe that spy-hopping allows these animals to get a good look at their surroundings. Whales may hang in this vertical position for a minute or more without falling over or sinking. The Gray Whale is known to assume this position to concentrate plankton collected on its baleen plates. Once the food is concentrated, it shakes its head, which allows the food to fall into its mouth. The spy-hopping position takes some effort to achieve; a 30- or 40-ton Gray Whale moves its tail through the water at speeds approaching 25 miles per hour in order to spy-hop.

Flipper Smacking and Fluke Smacking

Flipper smacking and fluke smacking, which are also known as "lob-tailing," may be a method of long-distance communication between individual or groups of whales. When either the flipper or the fluke is slightly cupped, the sound produced when it hits the water can be deafening, sometimes sounding almost like a cannon blast. The sound carries for miles underwater. Some

A Gray Whale "spy-hopping." The eyes are on the sides of its head, near the mouth.

researchers studying whale behavior have concluded that at times, whales smack their flippers and flukes just for fun.

Fluke Waving   Also known by sailors as "fluking up," fluke waving is performed by a number of the larger species of whales, including the Blue Whale *(Balaenoptera musculus)*, the Sperm Whale, the Right Whale, the Gray Whale, and the Humpback Whale. These whales raise their tail flukes vertically out of the water. One theory holds that fluke waving helps to orient a whale just before it dives. By lifting the tail out of the water, a whale may be able to shift its massive body so that its center of gravity is directed precisely downwards, making the dive nearly effortless for these large creatures. For whale watchers, fluke waving can be an easy preliminary method of identification, since not all whales do it. Scientists take advantage of fluke waving when studying Humpback Whales, since each individual of

A Humpback raises a flipper, ready to smack it on the water's surface.

this species has a distinctive pattern on its tail, which can help scientists to track individuals during long-term behavior and migration studies.

Sounding

Each species of whale has a distinctive method of sounding, or diving, after its periodic return to the surface of the water to breathe. Most whales take several breaths, then arch their backs and descend into the depths, raising their flukes as they dive. Some species, such as the Humpback Whale, the Gray Whale, and the Sperm Whale, lift their flukes nearly perpendicular to the surface of the water while sounding. The Gray Whale in particular holds its flukes high in the air before slipping down through the water. Some whales lift their flukes only slightly above the water's surface while sounding. Other species, such as Bryde's Whales *(Balaenoptera edeni)* and Sei Whales *(Balaenoptera borealis)*, do not raise their flukes above the surface at all.

A Gray Whale sounding.

Guide to Groups

The marine mammals included in this guide are assigned to several different orders, suborders, and families.

Whales, Dolphins, and Porpoises

Whales, dolphins, and porpoises belong to the order Cetacea. They have a fusiform body with paddle-shaped anterior flippers that evolved from mammalian forelegs. The posterior portion of the tail is flattened laterally to form horizontally flattened (depressed) flukes. Most cetaceans have a dorsal fin in the midline of the back.

Cetaceans are divided into two suborders, Mysticeti and Odontoceti. The mysticetes, or baleen whales, lack teeth but have plates of tough, horny baleen (whalebone) hanging down from the upper jaw. This suborder includes the Rorquals (Family Balaenopteridae), Right Whales (Family Balaenidae), and Gray Whales (Family Eschrichtidae).
The odontocetes, also known as toothed whales, have teeth, although the number varies among species. Odontocetes have a single blowhole (nostril). This suborder includes the Beaked Whales (Family Ziphiidae), Sperm Whales (Family Physeteridae), Narwhal and White Whales (Family Monodontidae),

Ocean Dolphins (Family Delphinidae), and Porpoises (Family Phocoenidae).

Seals, Sea Lions, and the Walrus	These aquatic carnivores, formerly placed in their own order Pinnipedia, meaning "fin feet," are believed to have evolved from the same ancestral groups as the bears and the mustelids. These animals are distinguished by adaptations for their aquatic life: torpedolike bodies; legs modified as flippers; and nostrils and ears, when present, that close when submerged.
	Eared Seals belong to the Family Otariidae and Earless Seals to the Family Phocidae; the Walrus is the only member of the Family Odobenidae
Sea Otters	The Sea Otter belongs to the Family Mustelidae. Members of this family include the arboreal Marten and the burrowing Badger. The Sea Otter's hindlegs are flipperlike, so it is clumsy on land.
Manatees	The Manatee belongs to the Order Sirenia, whose members are large, cylindrically shaped aquatic mammals that live in warm, shallow coastal waters or rivers. The Manatee belongs to the Family Trichechidae.

181

Parts of Whales

Baleen Whale

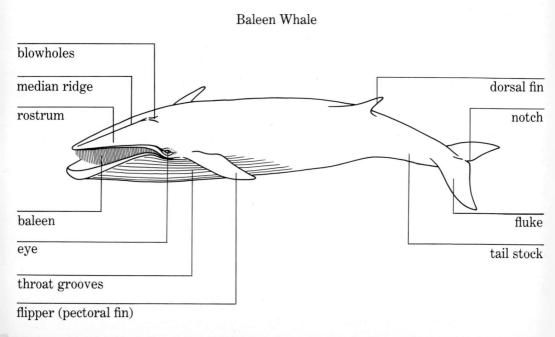

blowholes

median ridge

rostrum

dorsal fin

notch

baleen

eye

throat grooves

flipper (pectoral fin)

fluke

tail stock

Toothed Whale

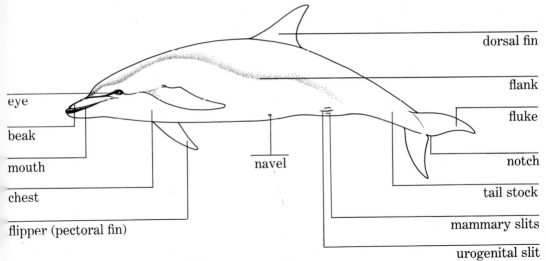

eye

beak

mouth

chest

flipper (pectoral fin)

navel

dorsal fin

flank

fluke

notch

tail stock

mammary slits

urogenital slit

Whale Diving Sequences

Certain species of whales have characteristic ways of sounding, or diving beneath the surface of the water, which can be used by whale watchers as a method of identification. Some species show most of their backs and throw their tails, or flukes, high in the air. Other species are less spectacular in their movements. Shown at right are the distinctive diving sequences of three species, the Humpback Whale, the Sperm Whale, and the Blue Whale. When making a deep dive, the Humpback Whale rounds its back above the surface of the water, then throws its flukes high in the air. The Sperm Whale rounds the entire rear part of its body into an arch, then raises its tail almost vertically, and lets it hang in the air for a moment before diving straight down. Blue Whales raise their flukes only slightly above the surface after rolling their long bodies through the water.

Humpback Whale

Sperm Whale

Blue Whale

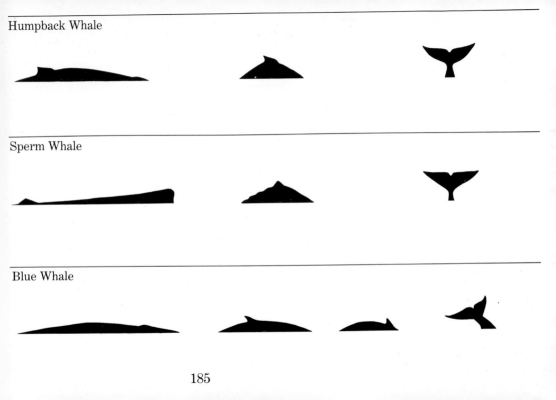

Glossary

Baleen
In some whales, the fibrous plates in parallel rows on each side of the upper jaw.

Band
A pigmented diagonal or oblique line.

Beak
In many toothed whales, the elongated forward portion of the head, consisting of the rostrum and the lower jaw.

Blow
In cetaceans, the expulsion of air at the surface through the blowhole(s), or nostril(s), during exhalation; also called the spout.

Blowhole
In cetaceans, the respiratory opening; single in toothed whales, paired in baleen whales.

Brackish
Slightly less salty than ordinary seawater.

Cetacean
Member of the Order Cetacea, which includes whales, dolphins, and porpoises.

Dorsal
Pertaining to the back or upper surface of the body.

Dorsal fin
The fin along the midline of the back, supported by rays; often notched or divided into separate fins.

Echolocation
The way in which certain animals orient themselves by emitting high-frequency sounds and interpreting the reflected sound waves.

Flippers
In cetaceans, the forelimbs.

Flukes
In cetaceans, the horizontally positioned tail fin; resembling the tail of a fish.

Fusiform
Spindle shaped or torpedo shaped; tapering toward ends.

Keel
A sharp ridge located, in some cetaceans, usually just in front of the flukes.

Krill
Small shrimplike crustaceans. An important part of the diets of many baleen whales.

Melon
In many toothed whales, the bulging forehead, often containing oil or spermaceti.

Pelagic
Living or growing near the surface of the sea.

Rookery
The breeding grounds of certain species of seals and the Walrus.

Rostrum
In cetaceans, a forward extension of the upper jaw. *Adj.* rostral.

Snout
The part of the head extending from the front margin of the eye to the forwardmost tip of the head.

Spout
A visible cloud expelled by a cetacean during exhalation at the water surface; also called the blow.

Ventral
Pertaining to the belly, underside, or lower part of the body.

Ventral grooves
In some baleen whales, the furrows extending backwards from the chin.

Index

Photographers

Peter Arnold, Inc.
Fred Bruemmer (155, 167),
Robert B. Evans (139),
Steve Kaufman (65),
C. Allan Morgan (159)

Fred Bruemmer (67)
E.R. Degginger (83, 145)

Earthviews
C. W. Oliver (75), Robert L.
Pitman (69, 85), Heinrich Schatz
(113), Richard Sears (107), James
D. Watt (115), John Woestendiel
(111)

Jeff Foott (27, 31, 51, 141)
François Gohier (49, 55, 61, 79, 81,
165, 175)
Daniel W. Gotshall (29)
Howard Hall (63)
Thomas Jefferson (105)
C. Allan Morgan (21, 77, 117, 179)
Sharon Nogg (103, 109, 161, 169,
173)

National Audubon Society
Collection/Photo Researchers, Inc.
William Curtsinger (37, 43, 73, 95,
171), Gregory G. Dimijian, M.D.
(25), Douglas Faulkner (47, 143),
Kenneth W. Fink (23), François
Gohier (59, 71), Robert Hernandez
(157), Tom and Pat Leeson (17),
Bud Lehnhausen (41), Tom
McHugh (35), Frank W. Mantlik
(93), G. Carlton Ray (33, 39, 97,
149), Jean-Philippe Varin/Jacana
(91)

Betty Randall (147, 151, 153)
Mari Ann Smultea (99, 177)

Valan Photos
Jeff Foott (45), W. Hoek (163),
John Johnson (19), M. Julien (87),
Richard Sears (53, 57, 89, 101)

Illustrators
Paintings by Larry Foster,
Earthviews (121-137)
Silhouettes by Paul Singer

Drawings by Dolores R.
Santoliquido and Paul Singer

Chanticleer Press
Publisher: Andrew Stewart
Senior Editor: Ann Whitman
Editor: Carol M. Healy
Project Editor: Ann ffolliott
Editorial Assistant: Kate Jacobs
Production: Kathy Rosenbloom,
Karyn Slutsky
Project Design: Paul Zakris
Photo Library: Tim Allan

Natural Science Consultant: John
Farrand, Jr.
Series Design: Massimo Vignelli

The Audubon Society

The NATIONAL AUDUBON SOCIETY, incorporated in 1905, is one of the oldest and largest conservation organizations in the world. Named after American wildlife artist and naturalist, John James Audubon, the Society has nearly 600,000 members in 500 chapters, nine regional and five state offices, as well as a government affairs center in Washington, D.C. Its headquarters are in New York City.

The Society works on behalf of our natural heritage through scientific research, environmental education, and conservation action. It maintains a network of almost 90 wildlife sanctuaries nationwide, conducts ecology camps for adults, and youth programs for schoolchildren. The Society publishes the leading conservation and nature magazine, *Audubon;* an ornithological journal, *American Birds;* and World of Audubon Television Specials, newsletters, video cassettes and interactive discs, and other educational materials.

For further information regarding membership in the Society, write to the NATIONAL AUDUBON SOCIETY, 950 Third Avenue, New York, N.Y. 10022.